henhouse

by Kaite O'Reilly

for Tatjana, Vesna, Branca, Durdica,
Andrea, Iskra and Sladjana. *Jivali!*

for Chris Katiæ, *with love*

henhouse

by Kaite O'Reilly

henhouse was first performed at the Arcola Theatre, London on 21 September 2004, with the following cast:

Mary Eileen Pollock
Hugh Gary Lilburn
Old Man Terry O'Brien
Young Man Celyn Jones
Young Woman Kate Drew

Directed by Bill Hopkinson
Designer Bronia Housman
Production Manager Deborah Metcalf-Askew
Lighting and Sound Chris Barham
Maker Sam Westbury

Produced by Bill Hopkinson and Celyn Jones
Press and Publicity Dan Pursey
danpursey@mobiusindustries.com
020 7731 1202

Thanks to

Iskra Pavloviæ, Radovan and Barbara Katiæ, Phillip Zarrilli, Alex Alderton, Sam Boardman Jacobs, Tony Brown, Louise Bush, David Ganly, Dyfrig Morris, Carri Munn, Mark McGann, Fred Ridgeway, Bill Wright, Chris O'Connell and The Writing House, Carl Proctor, Dr Nicola Shaughnessy, Professor Paul Allain, Sgript Cymru, Mai Jones, Simon Harris, Ted & Jean Hopkinson, William Forrest, Sian Stevenson, Rebecca Warren, Nina Wigfall, and to Bill and Paul Munsey, Wessex millers of Clarks (Wantage) Ltd. for their excellent bread flour.

Special thanks to the School of Drama, Film and Visual Arts, University of Kent without whose practical support this production would not have been possible.

The writing of this play was supported with a Playwrights' Bursary from the Arts Council of Wales in 2000.

Foreword

FOR SIX YEARS in the 1990s, my friend the writer Christina Katic and I were volunteers for Suncokret Humanitarian Relief Aid Agency, in former Yugoslavia. Through the civil war, during Operation Storm, and then through the painful years of post-war reconstruction, we worked with children and adults experiencing severe post-traumatic disorders, supporting local psychologists, teachers and social workers in frontline towns.

Kosovo, Rwanda, Srebrenica... I remember the 90s as being a time when the world seemed mad and out of control – it was better to be active, even at some personal risk, than frozen before the images flickering on TV. Besides, Chris and I had skills which were transferable, and in demand. So we went – and continued to return – staying in the same room in the Karlovac orphanage (all the hotels were bombed), working with the same colleagues, getting drunk with the same friends, watching the children become young adults, the bombed-out homes in the disputed Krajina being rebuilt, the family units trying to reassemble themselves...

There was a time of stasis, an exhausted drawing of breath. I also remember the reckoning: a dulled recounting of atrocities and crimes before recovery could begin. What struck me was the incredible effort required; the immense act of faith needed to rebuild splintered communities, to heal people who had witnessed or even perpetrated unimaginable acts on other human beings. 'We're fucked,' 17-year-old Sladjana wrote to me, 'there is something dark now in us. We have seen how things truly are, but perhaps that can save us... If this can happen here, it can happen anywhere.'

And she is right, of course, which is why *henhouse* is not set in former Yugoslavia, or the North of Ireland, or the West Bank, or...

But it begins, I think, at that moment of stasis, when family members fail to recognise one another, where dissolution is all around, where, given the right tending, the seeds of destruction might also be the source of redemption.

Kaite O'Reilly
Singapore, August 2004

Biographies

Eileen Pollock Mary

Eileen feels privileged to be working on her second Kaite O'Reilly play; her first was *Belonging* at Birmingham Rep. In 2003 she was in *Scenes From The Big Picture* at the Royal National Theatre; *Playboy of the Western World*, Royal Exchange, Manchester; and play-readings at the Royal Court. To date 2004 has been a less regal and more regional year, touring with the newly formed Association of Regional Theatres, Northern Ireland (ARTNI) in Adrian Dunbar's production of *Philadelphia, Here I Come!* Film credits within living memory are: *Far and Away*, Ron Howard; *Four Days in July*, Mike Leigh; *A Love Divided,* Sydney McCartney, *Wild About Harry*; Declan Lowney; *Angela's Ashes*, Alan Parker; and *Squaddie*, Conor McDermottroe. 'Off the television', Eileen is probably best known as Lilo Lil in Carla Lane's *Bread*. Radio work includes the titles roles in *Boudicca*, BBC London; and *The Pamela Mayers Show*, BBC Manchester. She has two one-woman shows: *Fight Like Tigers* drawn from the autobiography of the Irish-American mineworkers' leader, Mother Jones; and *Kathleen, Mother of all the Behans,* which she was invited to do by Brian Behan, brother of the possibly more infamous Brendan. Future bankruptcy projects include the staging of little-known Lady Gregory translations of Moliere scripts.

Gary Lilburn Hugh

Gary Lilburn trained at The Drama Centre, London. Recent Theatre Credits include: *The Quare Fellow* Oxford Stage Company; *A Midsummer Night's Dream* and *The Golden Ass*, Shakespeare's Globe; *Buried Alive*, Hampstead Theatre; *The Weir*, Royal Court; *Angels and Saints*, Soho Theatre; *Death of a Salesman* and *Dolly West's Kitchen*, Leicester Haymarket; *Desire Under the Elms*, Shared Experience; and *The Night Garden*, RNT Studio. He has had a long association with the New Victoria Theatre in Stoke, playing in 12 productions, among them: *Waiting for Godot, Candida, Way up Stream, Of Mice and Men,* and *Blood Knot.* Other theatre work includes: *Cat on a Hot Tin Roof*, Lyric, Belfast; *The Caretaker*, Sherman, Cardiff; *One Flew Over the Cuckoo's Nest,* West End; *Translations*, Theatr Clwyd; *The Beggar's Opera*, Druid; and *Three Sisters*, Field Day. Television work includes: Sea of Souls, 55 Degrees North, Grease Monkeys, The Bill, Dalziel and Pascoe, Eastenders, My Family, McCready and Daughter, Fair City, A Safe House, and Perfect Scoundrels. Film: Veronica Guerin.

Terry O'Brien Old Man

Read English & Drama at London University, later training at Guildhall. For over 30 years Terry has combined acting with teaching drama; former students include Fred Ridgeway, Romola Garai, composer Paddy Cunneen, and directors Toby Frow and Lucy Foster. Highlights of an extensive broadcasting career include a radio series on the Irish Famine, featuring Stephen Rea and Bob Geldof, and Margaret Percy's acclaimed docu-drama *Bloody Sunday*. Toured U.K. and Europe with own one-man show *Growing Pains* on Yeats, Joyce, & Brian Friel. With fellow actors Paulina Dare and Malcolm James devised, directed and toured *Love & Marriage*. Founder member, with Doris Daly and Shane Connaughton, of Irish Performing Arts Company, for whom he directed *The Countess Markiewicz* and *Who Fears To Speak* at Riverside Studios, followed by John Arden and Margaretta d'Arcy's *The Non-Stop Connolly Show* (U.K. tour). Recent credits include: Film & TV: The Incident; Pepper's Ghost; Bird of Prey; Crossfire; Midsomer Murders. Theatre: *The Tempest,* Almeida; *Christmas*, The Bush; *Car Thieves*, NT Studio & Cottesloe; *Whiskey in the Jar*, Andrews Lane Dublin.

Celyn Jones Young Man

Celyn was born and raised in Anglesey North Wales and trained at the Manchester Youth Theatre and then The Oxford School of Drama. He made his professional debut playing Henry Pratt in *Second From Last in the Sack Race* at the New Vic Theatre and has recently finished an International Tour of Gary Owen's *Ghost City* for Wales' national new writing theatre Sgript Cymru, which enjoyed great success off-Broadway prior to its London run. Other theatre credits include Matt in *Looking for K*, Soho Theatre: Mole in *Toad of Toad Hall*, New Vic, Stoke; Doc in *Confessional*, The Cockpit: Rudolph in *Cause Celebre*, BAC: Srulik in *Ghetto*, Library Theatre, Manchester; and the Grave Digger's Boy in Bond's *Lear*. Film and Television Credits include playing opposite Kenneth Branagh as Blackborow in Charles Sturridge's award-winning mini series *Shackleton*; Trevor in the BBC period drama *Hearts of Gold*; Mr Green in the children's drama *Grange Hill*; Rowan in BBC Wales's *The Bench* and Nick in *Stainless* for Mersey Film.

Kate Drew Young Woman

Kate grew up just outside of Liverpool and trained for 3 years at the Central School of Speech and Drama. Her credits include a Number 1 tour of *The Deep Blue Sea*, Theatre Royal Bath; Chorus in *Agamemnon*, Library Theatre (Best Production, Manchester Evening News Awards); and Susie in *Stainless*, Mersey Film. Kate is delighted that *Henhouse* will be her professional London Debut.

Kaite O'Reilly Playwright

Kaite's first London production won the Peggy Ramsay Award with *Yard*, translated as *Schlacthaus* it ran in rep at the Maxim Gorki Theatre, Berlin, for two years. She has had plays at the Bush, Contact Manchester, Birmingham Rep, and at the Royal Court as part the of Young Writers Festival with *Banshees*. Graeae Theatre Co. performed the triumphant *Peeling,* touring nationally and internationally, playing Soho Theatre in 2002, and the Assembly rooms Edinburgh in 2003. She is currently under commission from Sgript Cymru, Liverpool Biennial Live Art Festival, and Theatr Asou with a forthcoming production in Graz, Austria, and a residency in Singapore this summer.

Bill Hopkinson Director

Bill is an award-winning director (Manchester Evening News 1999, 2000) and teacher. For the last three years he has been part of the artistic team at Sgript Cymru, Wales. He has worked extensively as a dramaturg, developing new writing for the stage, including over a decade with Northwest Playwrights. As director he has premiered new plays by Christina Katic, Mike Mallet and Alan Williams; recent work includes devised projects for Commonground Sign Dance Theatre, and the Sherman Theatre, Cardiff, and *Looking for K* by Danny Start, (Soho Theatre/Graeae/Writernet). He has collaborated with Kaite O'Reilly on many projects over an 18 year period, including the British premiere of her play *Banshees*. They regularly teach courses together at the national Welsh writing centre, Ty Newydd. Bill is Artistic Director of Glossolalia.

Bronia Housman Designer

Bronia trained at the Motley Theatre Design Course in London after gaining a Drama & Theatre Studies degree from the University of Kent. Designs include: an independent short film, *November Sky*; *Between Two,* Bonnie Bird Theatre at Laban Centre; *After Sex All The Animals Are Sad*, Hoxton Hall, London and Edinburgh Fringe; *Christie in Love*, Lumley Studio, Canterbury; *Reaching for the Blue Star Sky*, Aphra Theatre, Canterbury; *Fall of the House of Usher* and *Waste,* both Gulbenkian Theatre, Canterbury. Recently she collaborated with facing/the/crowd on *Oral and Bill*, an installation in a beach hut in Whitstable. Bronia is currently designing 6 touring shows for White Horse Theatre in Germany.

Glossolalia means 'speaking in tongues'. We are a new theatre company devoted to making thought-provoking, exciting European theatre, which involves playwrights, directors and actors in an equal process of creation across divides of language, culture and practice. We aspire to create work which is unashamedly political, passionate, contemporary and human.

arcola
theatre

'This is real theatre, poor but purposeful, rooted in its community but speaking to everyone.' *The Sunday Times*

Founded in September 2000 by its present artistic director Mehmet Ergen, the Arcola began life in a converted textile factory on the borders of Stoke Newington and Dalston, one of London's most deprived areas with the highest concentration of artists living anywhere in Europe, yet no venue to give that creative output space and support. Today our spacious premises boast one of London's largest and most adaptable fringe spaces. Arcola Theatre consistently aims to create and present theatre performances and events of high quality with a social, economical and political relevance not only to a general audience but also in particular to its multi-cultural community in which we take an active involvement.

In just four years Arcola has become one of the country's fastest growing fringe venues. Awarded a Peter Brook Empty Space Award for the second year running as well as a Time Out Live Award 2003; some of the UK's best new writers and directors (John Retallack, Bonnie Greer and David Farr to name but a few) have injected considerable time and energy into productions. Every show maintains consistently high standards of social accessibility and of gritty, political relevance.

Characters

MARY

HUGH

OLD MAN

YOUNG MAN

YOUNG WOMAN

The action takes place in the farmhouse kitchen
of a subsistence-farming family

Scene 1
Present

Scenes 2–4
Nine months earlier,
played sequentially over a week

Scenes 5–6
Twenty months earlier than Scene 1

It is played in reverse chronology. It starts in the present and ends two years earlier. The play moves from disintegration and fragmentation toward a more everyday orderliness.

This is reflected in the set and physical appearance of the characters. At first the kitchen is dilapidated and bare, the characters worn and in old, unlaundered clothes. The action revolves backwards to slightly better, more peaceful times, signified by the improving quality of human welfare and material things.

Although all the characters in the play are 'a family' – this is intentionally not made specific or explicit throughout the play. By the end of the piece, it should be apparent that this 'random' group of people are related. It is important in production that the actors clearly play each scene and action on its own terms and without reference to their role within this 'family' so that the relationships between these characters remain open to interpretation until the closing.

To be played without interval.

1

The present

A dilapidated kitchen in a farmhouse, without mains power. Strategically-placed hurricane lamps and candles provide light, a wood-burning stove supplies heat. HUGH, a middle-aged man, sits alone, hunched over a small old-fashioned record player. He looks unwashed, neglected. He fiddles with wires connected to a charged car battery beside him. Faintly, tinnily, the strains of Maria Callas singing rise up from the stereo. The volume is low, barely audible. HUGH leans over hungrily, the better to absorb the music, but also to hide his action. He should not be wasting the battery so – he knows it but cannot help himself. He listens. Every fibre in his body listens.

Time passes.

The outside door slams. He hurriedly switches off the stereo, unhooks it from the battery and covers it up with a heavy cloth. He sits.

A woman, MARY, enters. Her hair is scraped back off her face, covered with a rag; she is dirty from the land. She discards her worn man's oversized coat and muddy rubber boots. Without thinking, she crosses to wash her hands at the sink. She turns on the tap but no water flows out. She remembers there is no mains supply, goes to an old pitcher in the corner, pours water into a bowl, washes herself ineffectually. HUGH sits.

MARY: That creature's back.

> *Silence.*

All but sitting there, bold as brass, looking at me.

> *She looks at HUGH. No response.*

Staring me out. Defying.

HUGH: Did you see it, then?

MARY: No.

I was just saying, it was all but –

HUGH: – Did it take many?

MARY: One.

HUGH: Are the others dead?

She gestures they are still alive. HUGH sits. MARY busies herself. Silence.

Stoat.

MARY: I said it was the –

HUGH: – Stoat. A fox'd take the lot. Kill them all. Flurry. Has no eye for the future. Feast today, tomorrow a –

MARY: – Fox.

HUGH: Did you see it?

MARY: No.

HUGH: A pole cat, then.

MARY: I said –

HUGH: – Weasel. Stoat. A fox'll –

MARY: – Will you have a cup of tea?

HUGH: Are you making a real pot?

Pause.

MARY: Bags.

Pause.

HUGH: I won't.

MARY: Are you sure now?

HUGH: Not if you're not making a real pot, no.

MARY fills the kettle, puts it on the wood-burning stove. A beat.

HUGH: Couldn't we have a real pot?

MARY: Bags is easier.

HUGH: It'd be a nice change. A proper one. Loose tea.

MARY: It's the mess…

HUGH: But I do taste the paper on them bag things.

MARY: …I haven't all day to be swilling round the sink for them gobshitey tealeaves…

HUGH: In a nice warmed pot, scalded first to bring out the flavour.

MARY: …Some of them are as big as communion wafers and the rest is all dust.

HUGH: Could I not have proper tea? For a change?

MARY: If so, you may make it yourself. And buy it, too, for I won't have that in my cupboards. It's me who has to clean them out, not you. It's a waste to the day.

Silence.

HUGH: Aw, go on, then. I'll have an oul rag.

Silence.

MARY: Round, square, or the nice pyramids?

HUGH: The Egyptian one. I do like to have a little mystery to me tea.

MARY: I'll make a proper pot then.

She begins making the tea with loose leaves. HUGH is silent with satisfaction. A pause.

HUGH: So it's back, then. The creature.

MARY: Four of my bantams gone and it not yet Christmas.

HUGH: Did you put the galvanised over the door, like I told you?

MARY: Shut tight and bolted.

HUGH: I never knew of a creature that could slide back a bolt, then lock it up tidy, after.

MARY: Yes you do.

A beat.

HUGH: Ah, there's many get cunning in the wild. Now, a stoat. A stoat'd –

MARY stops in the process of bringing him his tea.

Did you see the fox?

She decides to bring him the tea. She sits, on a hard back chair. Silence as they enjoy their tea.

D'you know what I was thinking about the other day?

She shakes her head, waits for an answer, it doesn't come. They stir their tea in silence. Several beats.

Anything happen, then?

MARY: No.

HUGH: Today. When you were out in the fields.

She shakes her head.

The world?

MARY: No.

HUGH: Nothing?

MARY: At all.

HUGH: Except the creature.

MARY: That was yesterday.

He looks at her, affronted.

I don't have to tell you everything.

Pause.

There was a bit of plastic caught in the barbed wire up where Mahoney's* used to be.

HUGH: The top field?

MARY: No, across over past the hen house. Near the ditch.

HUGH: Wasn't that the Conlan's?

MARY: Thirty-five years ago. The Hanratteys bought it from the Conlans who lost it out to Mahoney. Ministry of Defence has it now.

HUGH: So nothing's grown on it?

MARY: Not a sot.
I thought it was a blackbird, an oul crow, y'know, a raven. Walked the length of the field and it was a bit of polythene.

HUGH: Caught up on the barbed wire, you say? Recent?

MARY: Probably there months. Got blown over from them bad winds we had not long ago.

HUGH: A good size of polythene, or just a scrap?

MARY: In between.

HUGH: Was it dirty, like it'd been used, or brand new?

MARY: Hard to tell.

---

* Surnames appropriate to the production's context may be inserted in lieu of those used here.

HUGH: Oh.
It's a waste.
That land used to be a lovely field. God, the grass you'd
get on it. As green as… Feed a herd of cows, and more.

MARY: It's still there.
The grass.
A bit of weed amongst it. Piss the Bed. Cattle cabbage.

HUGH: D'you remember the day the Mother served up
that broccoli with the Sunday dinner and the old man
throwing the plate out of the door, saying he wouldn't
eat nothing that a beast with three stomachs does. Said
he didn't have the constitution nor the equipment for it
and them hens there pecking away, becoming carnivores,
with the Mother's best lamb and mint sauce on the
flagstones. And then him bawling and beseeching,
threatening to wring their necks for them being so
unnatural and eating the meat, d'you remember?

Silence.

You do, you did, aw – maybe I imagined it.

They finish their tea.

MARY: They say a black bird about the house is fierce
unlucky.
Brings death. And disease. Foreboding.
But no, not at all, just a piece of old plastic.
D'you want a top up?

HUGH: I thought you said it was polythene.

MARY: One of them.

HUGH: But there's a world of difference between plastic
and polythene.

MARY: It was one of them, anyway.

HUGH: But which?

MARY: (*Generously.*) You decide.
Now.

She takes the empty cups and tidies them away. She returns and sits on the hard chair. They wait in silence.

HUGH: Would you not want to make yourself comfortable?

MARY: I'm grand.

She repositions herself on the chair, clasps her hands. They wait. He looks at her hands. She becomes aware of his scrutiny

I do have to hold them in my lap otherwise they'd be up, looking for something to do.

HUGH: Finding mischief, ha?

She does not respond. Silence. They listen to it.

It does get quiet, now, of an evening.

MARY: Indeed. I was only thinking to myself the other day: 'these evenings now, they're very quiet'.

HUGH: Not like the summer.

MARY: Not at all like the summer.

HUGH: It does be noisy then.
The sun deafening as it pours onto the flags.

MARY: Ah, it makes a sound all right.

HUGH: You miss it. When it gets dark. When the back end draws in. You'd be cursing it in the summer, desperate for a little peace and quiet, and when it comes...

MARY: The silence is deafening.

HUGH: Still, it's good to have a bit of company, ha?

MARY: Indeed.

HUGH: A bit of a chat in the evening, no?
Chewing the fat.
Sharing the day.
Life, ha?

Silence. They sit, vaguely nodding at each other. Several beats.

MARY gets up and searches for something in various cupboards and boxes.

HUGH: I'm been wanting to ask – that is, after seeing you today out there in the fields –
Do we have any seed, Mary?

MARY finds a large tapestry sewing bag and takes it neatly to her hard back chair. She sorts through it.

It was just I got a glance of you out there, forehead down, steering into the wind –

MARY: – Aw, it was mighty.

HUGH: I thought as much. I could tell as much from the window. I got a glance of you from there, bent double, forcing against the wind. Were you able to make a furrow?

MARY: Not so you'd notice, but there's no harm in trying.

HUGH: There is not.

MARY: And a field needs to be ploughed.

MARY takes out a large white cloth and begins embroidering it.

HUGH: So do we? Have any seed?

MARY: We do in me tail.

HUGH: No little germ, or grain?

MARY: None.

HUGH: A sapling? Pod, even?

MARY: Neither.

HUGH: So there's nothing to plant?

MARY: Not a thing.

HUGH: Not a sot to sow?

MARY: No.

HUGH: Though you wouldn't let a fact like that stop you?

MARY: I would not. The earth does be hungry. It needs to be tended.

HUGH: I saw you out there, forehead down, shoulders bent against the wind.

MARY: Aw, it was mighty.

HUGH: I heard tell of a breeze that can blow a man's brains clean away. All the sense in his head, caught up in the howl. Never the same, after. Maddened.

MARY: Trample it down, trample, like a nettle underfoot. You'd trample on a nettle, wouldn't you?

HUGH: I would.

MARY: So trample on this. Thinking. Being morbid. There's no cure in that stinger's bed. Just barbs. And pain. Would you want that?

HUGH: No.

MARY: So trample. And be still.

A pause.

HUGH: That's a lovely cloth you're embroidering.

MARY: It is not.

HUGH: An altar cloth is it Mary? For an altar?

She does not answer.

And what was the wind doing? Today, when you were abroad in the fields?
I got a glance of you from the window, bent double on yourself, steering into the gale. Was that wind bad?

MARY: Terrible fierce.

HUGH: But there's no seed, you say?
Ah, perhaps it's not needed.

MARY: The earth does not forget.

HUGH: It doesn't.

MARY: It remembers its tending and misses it when it's gone. So I don't. Miss it, that is. I tend, I look after my own.

Pause.

Though it does be hard without the horse.

Pause.

The plough has no power. No force to it whatsoever.

Pause.

I do feel like I'm pushing an oul pram with a blade underneath.
Imagine!

Pause.

But the soil does be grateful and we'll reap our reward.

HUGH: An empty harvest.

MARY: It does the soil good. And we will benefit. You mark my words. The moon goes down and the sun rises. It happens every morning. I see it. I watch. And it has never failed me yet. Like that field. The stomachs that have been made full because of that field! And I tend it. And it will yield up shoots. Like the sun going round, golden stalks where once there was clay.

HUGH: But Mary, if we have no –

MARY: – Are you doubting me? And that fine, good field?

HUGH: Mary –

MARY: Are you?

HUGH: Mary, have you ever thought of getting help with the ploughing? A strong one in harness, tugging away.

MARY: Sweet Jesus, where would we find –

HUGH: – That year when I a boy and the Mother strapped in, pulling. The old man behind roaring at her to giddy up and the reins lashing, cutting into her skin and him heaving behind her, the soil torn, turning in on itself like a slug under salt. And her weeping and on her knees but she wouldn't give in, she wouldn't and her tugging up and down down and up all day that one field and he wouldn't stop nor give her water till they'd finished and they did. Finish. Finished it. The field. That rich dark soil, like the Christmas pudding she did make, so rich and moist you'd want to put a crumb of it in your mouth and we did, that year they took the harvest, her boiling up the pots of the good earth and we eating it and grateful and glad for it and saying amen before we took up our spoons. So did you ever think of it, did you? Of putting a young one in harness?

MARY: And where would I find one of them?

HUGH: The young one – the young – the –

MARY: Haven't I enough yet with calluses on my hands
without going round looking for a –

HUGH: – Young one, that young one, the –
I've been dreaming again.

MARY: I keep telling you to stop but do you heed me? I
know when you're doing it, I can tell. I have ears on my
head and eyes in the skull, can all but feel it out in the
field the moment you're doing it. And will you ever
stop? Will you?

*The YOUNG WOMAN enters and crosses to the stove. She is
unkempt, dragging her body through the motions as she takes
up the pot from beneath a cloth and pours three cups of tea.
There is something defeated about her, her feet barely rising
from the floor as she brings the tea to MARY and HUGH.
Without expression she exits, taking her own cup with her.
MARY and HUGH do not acknowledge her, but drink the
tea contemplatively.*

A beat.

That tea's stewed. It's stood too long.

End of scene.

2

Nine months earlier.

The scenes follow sequentially until Scene 5.

The kitchen is not so untidy or neglected – a television sits on the side, the car battery, hurricane lamps and candles are gone – the house has electricity. All wear clothing that is old, but clean.

OLD MAN lies in a makeshift bed upstage left, eyes closed, the covers drawn up to his chin. MARY is kneading dough, making bread. YOUNG WOMAN appears by the door, she and MARY appraise each other warily before she enters. There is a sense YOUNG WOMAN has recently arrived – and not necessarily by invitation – but acts with the calm confidence of one with a natural right to be there, a right MARY seems to respect. She begins preparing her breakfast.

YOUNG WOMAN: Milk?

MARY: Fridge?

She looks in the fridge and takes out a pitcher of milk.

YOUNG WOMAN: Butter?

MARY: Same?

She looks in fridge and takes out a butter dish.

YOUNG WOMAN: Bread?

MARY: Making it.

YOUNG WOMAN: None?

MARY: Stale.

YOUNG WOMAN: Tea?

MARY: I'd love a cup.

YOUNG WOMAN: Tea?

MARY: Cupboard?

She takes out a caddy from the cupboard.

YOUNG WOMAN: Spoons?

MARY: Jesus, would you like me to drink it for you as well?

YOUNG WOMAN: Spoons?

MARY: Ah, gauge it, throw an oul handful in. (*Beat.*) That's the trouble with you young ones, useless without the tools. I'd like to see you washed up on a desert island. (*Beat.*) Wouldn't last two ticks. (*Beat.*) Would be looking for the tin opener to split the coconut –

The YOUNG WOMAN finds a spoon.

YOUNG WOMAN: – Sugar?

MARY: In the bloody cupboard!

YOUNG WOMAN faces MARY, showing she has the bowl in her hands.

Are you asking me if I take it?

The YOUNG WOMAN is impassive.

Are you?
(*Defeated.*) Four.
It does me good. The doctor as much as told me so.
A little bit of sweetness in a life does no harm.
Perhaps it does you no good, either.
Makes you want things.
Comfort.
Well that's what it is, I mean it is, it is to me, that is. A comfort. Indeed.
And a little bit of comfort, it can, it can, yes. Yes.
What did you say your name was again?

The YOUNG WOMAN does not answer. She brings the mug of tea to MARY and sits on the chair to take her own. The OLD MAN opens his eyes and fixes his gaze unblinking on the ceiling.

I like to take my elevenses at nine. Gives you more time in the day. You can get ahead of yourself then.

Pause. They drink their tea.

I was called after the virgin. Odd that, when you think how I was beget. But there you go. No explanation. No logic to it at all. And it's best not thinking. I mean, if we were meant to be thinking more we'd be doing it, wouldn't we?
If it was meant. That is.
Something distinctive was it? Or, or more common?
The name?
I'm nearly certain that you whispered it, but ah, now, must've been the wind. A little mouse, ha, squeaking in the wainscot? Would you like me to wash your hair?

Pause.

Once the flour's off my hands, that is. I have a lovely way with the scalp.

Pause.

A good scratching, loosening your cares.
All the grime and bother just floating away.

No?

Pause.

Maybe later, when you're settled.

Pause.

Sometimes the Christmas is come and gone before I realise. The new year in and not so much as a resolution

made. He likes it. Puts up a sprig of holly and a twist of bacofoil but I pay no attention. It does no good to be encouraging them. You'd be giving them ideas and there's no saying where that all ends. A one-way ticket to trouble, you mark my words.
So don't go asking me about it now, I do be that busy with all the things to fit in a day I wouldn't notice when you come.
I wouldn't know when.
So.

MARY puts the bread in the oven and swills her mug under the tap. The water mains are now working. She pulls on men's boots, a cow gown and leather jerkin, all too big for her, and leaves.

YOUNG WOMAN sits. The OLD MAN takes his glance from the ceiling and settles it on her. She does not look. A pause.

YOUNG WOMAN: There was a robin at the side of the road, pecking at bushes. A woman, some time ago, told me they were lucky. As I drew near I saw it was a sparrow, its breast splattered with blood.

The OLD MAN closes his eyes. The YOUNG WOMAN sits.

A beat.

HUGH enters, rubbing his hands together. He is more sprightly than in Scene 1, his appearance less unkempt. He sees the YOUNG WOMAN and stops. He is surprised but cautious.

HUGH: Well well well.

They look at each other.

YOUNG WOMAN: You don't take sugar in your tea, do you?

She gets up and pours him a mug. He watches her, still. She brings it to him, encouraging him to sit in the armchair.

The bread's in the oven, the cow in her stall and all's right with the world you're not sleeping well.

HUGH: How? –

YOUNG WOMAN: – The shadows under your eyes. That's burst blood vessels. You want to watch that. Don't want to end up like a bloodhound Deputy Dawg shall I do the usual?

HUGH: The? –

YOUNG WOMAN: – What I always do. The custom. Our little ritual, event, practice, habit, you know.

HUGH: Our? –

YOUNG WOMAN: – Routine, tradition, observance, rite. It's not like you to make me have to offer it. Sell my wares so to speak. It doesn't make me look decorous.

HUGH: Dec-?

YOUNG WOMAN: – Dignified, becoming, mannerly, decent. 'You are lacking in decorum,' that is, in etiquette, proper behaviour, form.
'My dear, your actions last night were far from ladylike.'
Did I do it well? (*A beat.*)
Did you like it? (*A beat.*)
I learnt at least seven definitions and some examples of usage. After all, a man without mastery of language is master of nothing. Who said that?

He stares at her. She playfully scolds him.

You, silly.
You can have your tea now.

She pushes the mug up to his lips.

Because you've been a good boy, I'll allow you a spoon of honey.

She mimes spooning honey into his cup.

But it's not real honey of course, just pretend. The hive was empty when the bees flew away.
Shall I check the bread?

HUGH: Mary – it's Mary's –

YOUNG WOMAN: – Job? Not necessarily when I'm here. Look: I can walk across to the oven – see? Shall I peep in and see if the yeast is working? We'll scold it if it's flat, or shall we scold Mary? Who do you think is to blame?

HUGH: I –

YOUNG WOMAN: – Perhaps… Perhaps there's none in there. Perhaps…we only imagine we can smell the bread cooking and really the oven's bare. Can an oven be bare or is that just a cupboard?

HUGH: I don't know.

YOUNG WOMAN: I think we're dreaming.

Do you dream?

HUGH shakes his head.

Perhaps it's only possible when I'm here.

Stillness for a while.

You're not drinking your tea.

HUGH: I –

YOUNG WOMAN: Didn't you like it? Perhaps it stood too long.

HUGH: It's fine.

*He drains the mug. She watches him as he drinks, wiping his
lips with the back of his hand.*

All gone.

YOUNG WOMAN: Good.
I know how you like your tea in the morning.
It sets you up, doesn't it, for the rest of the day?

*HUGH sits in the chair, nodding. She sits on another chair,
nodding back. OLD MAN suddenly opens his eyes. As he
speaks, HUGH and YOUNG WOMAN's lines slightly
overlap his.*

OLD MAN: One foot in front of the other, another foot
before the other, step, step, lightly step plod.

HUGH: We found him out in the old hen house.

OLD MAN: One foot, the other foot, one foot soft to the
earth, step, move, step forward now not long. Stand.
Breathe.

HUGH: Rolled up he was, half frozen, three quarters dead
and not a ha'penny to his name.
If he has one.

OLD MAN: One foot crosses the other, another foot before
the other, step, breathe, step foot plod.

YOUNG WOMAN approaches the OLD MAN.

YOUNG WOMAN: He likes me.

OLD MAN: One foot before the other, next foot in front of
the other, heart flutters little bird, step step plod.

YOUNG WOMAN: He does.

OLD MAN: Breath breath breathe breath,

HUGH: Mary thought he was a fox, ready to pin him with
a pitchfork. But since when did they sprout poetry? Or at
least, that's what I said.

OLD MAN: heart bangs, bone cage, heart flutters, little bird. Note, hot pulse. Song, red thread. One foot in front of the other, another foot before the other, step, step, lightly step stop.

HUGH: Strangest looking fox I ever did see. But then, I've not been out much in the world. Have you?

A beat.

YOUNG WOMAN: See how he's gone quiet.

HUGH: Aw, we do that well enough here. Quiet. So quiet at times you can hear your skin ageing.

YOUNG WOMAN: He's looking at me.

HUGH: Have you? Travelled?

YOUNG WOMAN: Some.

HUGH: Seen the world?

YOUNG WOMAN: A bit.

HUGH: So it's still there.

YOUNG WOMAN: Just.
I didn't like it so I came back.

She looks at the OLD MAN.

I think we should shave him. He didn't used to have whiskers.

HUGH: How do –

YOUNG WOMAN: – By the way the stubble's growing. It's not comfortable with being that length. It's used to being shorn back twice a day. I can tell.
Do you have any soap?

HUGH: Plenty, but no blades.

HUGH fetches a mug of lathered soap, with shaving brush.

Mary doesn't allow anything sharp in the house.
She has the carving knife out hidden in the fields, in case
she needs it if they come. It does be covered in muck
when she carves the chicken on a meat Sunday. Maybe
she has it in the ditch.

*YOUNG WOMAN lathers up OLD MAN who begins to
protest at her handling.*

YOUNG WOMAN: It doesn't matter, I'll use my finger.

HUGH: I think she thinks that if they come they'll think
she's unarmed in the fields –

OLD MAN: Stop stop stop the –

YOUNG WOMAN: Ssssh.

HUGH: – And if they come to the house first, they'll find
no weapons.

OLD MAN: Stop the step, stop –

YOUNG WOMAN: Hush, now.

HUGH: For I would imagine they get through them pretty
quick. Metal blunts. And a blade needs to be steeled
otherwise it gets dull and when would they find the time
to be whittling?

OLD MAN: Stop, stop –

*YOUNG WOMAN starts using her finger on his neck and
cheeks as though it were a razor. She wipes the foam on to a
rag.*

YOUNG WOMAN: I'll make you nice and clean.

HUGH: Them off on the road and the dangerous living and
all. I've heard tell of them going through a house like a
swarm of ants, leaving nothing but the furniture in

33

matchsticks behind them. There'd be no chance at borrowing a steel to sharpen a blade then, would there?

OLD MAN: Stop the stop the –

YOUNG WOMAN: Ssssh.

HUGH: So the blades were the first to go.

OLD MAN: Stop the step the stop the –

She puts her mouth close to his ear and whispers.

YOUNG WOMAN: (*Menacingly.*) I hear the sound of feet going stamp, stamp, stamp – but nobody's there…

She holds her finger to his throat like a razor.

Cut throat. Shall we give your neck a smile?

The OLD MAN is immediately silent, as is HUGH, who watches her as she finishes the shave. She wipes off any excess foam from his face, admiring her handiwork.

There! You could almost imagine it shaved!

MARY enters with a clatter. She stands still, looking at them for a moment before rushing to the oven.

MARY: And did none of you think of checking the good bread and it spoiled!?

She throws a blackened loaf on to the table.

There it is and may you well eat it, for there's not enough flour to be squandering and throwing it away.

MARY looks at HUGH.

And what are you doing up, standing, wasting them legs? Indeed, I wasn't out on my knees pulling along that plough with me teeth for you to be stood on your feet, spoiling them.

MARY sees the cloth in YOUNG WOMAN's hands.

And that's my best rag. I'll be requesting that you use your own in future.

She snatches it from her and smoothes it out.

I've been keeping that for years, since my little –

She stops and looks at HUGH.

HUGH: Careful, now.

MARY: Since. My.

HUGH: Trample it down, Mary, trample.

MARY: My –

HUGH: Don't.

MARY: You made a tree house in the garden for the two of them and I'd take up little jam tarts, blowing on that wrinkled surface so it didn't scald when they bit into them...

HUGH: Mary...

MARY: ...And there was a basket they'd let down, tied to the rope she'd use for skipping and my heart was full to bursting although the world was full of sharp edges and jaggedness that I longed to save them from. But then you – indeed you did – you said that the world was a hard place and it was no good, no good would come from it at all, if I wrapped them in paper like the apples to last the winter. Lay them in the attic, beneath the cracked, sloping window with the smells of autumn and plenty, and an eiderdown of padding to protect from the bruise. So I didn't. I did not.
And they grew crooked and tardy; limped when they walked and their heads not held high. And I forgave you, indeed I did, I forgave you, when I still loved you that is, for you didn't know, you were just a man. And how is

a man expected to know such things? So I forgave you, whilst I still loved you, but then one day I stopped loving.
How's a body expected to carry on?
Ha?
But we do, we do.
So.

She looks at the YOUNG WOMAN.

I'll wash your hair, now.

YOUNG WOMAN: Yes.

Fifteen second blackout.

Later.

OLD MAN asleep in the makeshift bed. YOUNG WOMAN leans back on a chair, as MARY washes her hair in a bowl on the table.

MARY: Boyfriends?

YOUNG WOMAN: No.

MARY: Husband?

YOUNG WOMAN: Never!

MARY: I always thought Anne a nice name.

Pause.

A lover, then?

Pause.

There's no confusion with it. Simple. Clean. Not a name you can forget or make a mistake with and there's enough to be occupying a mind without having to remember what to call a body. Is that nice now?

Pause.

YOUNG WOMAN: One.

MARY: Only?

YOUNG WOMAN: Two.

MARY: Hhmmm…

YOUNG WOMAN: Twelve. More. A lot.

Though I didn't want them all. But to be given has less power than to steal.

MARY: Indeed, it's better to offer, for they will, you know, they'll only take.

YOUNG WOMAN: A woman taught me that, a long time ago. But I can't remember.

MARY: I always thought Anne a good name.

YOUNG WOMAN: Precise but general.

MARY: Ha?

YOUNG WOMAN: Anne Object.

MARY starts rinsing the suds off YOUNG WOMAN's hair.

MARY: My young one now, she had hair like yours. But lighter, maybe. Glossier. I think a bit more fine. But, ah, what do I know? I'm only inventing. She's long gone.

A pause.

YOUNG MAN stands in the doorway, holding a dead chicken by its feet. He is filthy, as is the worn, faded khaki shirt and combat trousers he wears.

There is a wildness about him.

YOUNG WOMAN: There's a man at the door.

MARY begins massaging YOUNG WOMAN's scalp, rinsing with fresh water from a jug.

MARY: Is it nice, is that now, is it? Them lovely claws in at your head? It's been many a year since I had these hands in warm water. I'm spoiling you. You're making me soft. Cold water doesn't waste the soap. You can never get a lather up and that's how I make things last. Same with the eggs.

YOUNG WOMAN: There's a man at the door.

MARY: I do see him but I imagine if we ignore him he'll go away. Keep the eggs warm in a pocket and they may hatch. Brassiere is better but I keep breaking them. Yolk all down the front. Terrible waste. I do try and scrape it off to make a scramble, but it always tastes of sweat.

The YOUNG MAN reaches forward, grabbing some bread. He holds it, watching as MARY squeezes the water from YOUNG WOMAN's hair.

He's welcome to the few things we have, if the food doesn't stick in his throat that is, thieving from them that have little enough as it is. But, ah, now, he's welcome to it so long as he comes and goes easy and doesn't break the old sticks of furniture.

MARY wraps YOUNG WOMAN's hair up into a towel as the MAN breaks off some of the bread.

I'm wondering if he's with others or all on his lonesome.

He chokes, coughing out the dry bread.

I imagine it must be parching on them dusty roads. There's enough tea in the pot for another and his name's on it so long as he doesn't use the best cups.

He moves slowly, cautiously over to the sideboard.

And there's not a knife in the house. They're all buried out in the field.

He turns his back to pour himself the tea. MARY strikes him over the head with the jug. He collapses, knocked out.

Now.

She crosses to the makeshift bed, pulling back the covers on the OLD MAN, revealing he is tightly bound with rope.

He's harmless.

She unties some of the rope and crosses back to the YOUNG MAN. The YOUNG WOMAN helps her to drag him into a sitting-up position. They bind him, hand to foot.

He has the stench of the world about him.

YOUNG WOMAN: All those mewling mouths, open with want. Fingers like little fish hooks, catching at your clothes, snagging in your skin, pulling, tugging, 'I want, I want.' The need!
There was a family camped at the side of the road – camped isn't the word. Thrown, more like. Collapsed. Legs giving in, falling down in the clothes they stood up in and I asked them, 'Why don't you go home?' but they looked at me like I spoke another language. 'Home', I said, but they didn't understand the word, it was old, outside their vocabulary, a definition didn't exist in their dictionary. So I repeated it and one laughed and said burning. Gone.

MARY: Ah, he has the stench all right.

YOUNG WOMAN: It's always the quiet ones to watch. Snapped tight, closed in on themselves, dangerous. Conserving all energy, limbs loose but bone brittle, waiting. You look in their eyes but the lights are out and no one's at home. They're hidden down, deep in the cellar with the spiders and the dark and half a village. No food. The suffering immeasurable. So still you can see a slug track across their hand. An army of snails. Legion. Not wanting anything but for it to end.

So I came back.

MARY: And I washed your hair.

They look at one another. MARY smoothes her hand over YOUNG WOMAN's head.

Anne is a good name.

End of scene.

3

A day later.

HUGH sits watching a recording of a concert performance by Maria Callas, Hamburg 1959, on the small black and white television. Blandly he reads aloud the subtitles of the impassioned libretto across the bottom of the screen. YOUNG WOMAN is finishing feeding YOUNG MAN, spooning soup into his mouth. He is still bound, but his face and hands have been wiped clean. When the bowl is empty, she moves away, starts plucking the chicken of Scene 2.

Several beats.

The volume of the opera reduces. HUGH continues reading the translation, his mouth silently shaping the text.

YOUNG MAN: There were four of us – Malachy, Pavlovic and the Greek. They called us the United fucking Nations. It was after the last time, that's when I – Four of us. Used kerosene. Old fashioned. Drag a mattress into the main room – horse hair – still burns – Malachy splashing the stuff all over the bloody place, running down his arms. Singed the hair off, later. Said that'd teach him, he'd learn. Never fucking did. Smell of pork, burning. I left then. Nothing to it. Change of clothes, plenty on the road, nearly ended up in a collective centre but carried on, due North, North West. Never had a compass, just walked, followed my nose, smelt my way. Easy. Could have passed as one of them. Often did. Any sign of trouble and I'd just open my mouth and they heard. 'Oh.' Good as a passport, better. Doesn't get wet when you swim.

HUGH: I never could see what she did in Onasis.

YOUNG MAN: You help yourself to houses along the way. It's not stealing. I'm no thief. Nothing fucking left, anyway. Looted already, the lads before me. See them walking up the road with a telly on their head. Video.

CD. Sometimes they'll take the cooker if they've wheels, don't bother with disconnecting, just rip it out, toss a match and there she blows.

HUGH: And Mary says she sounds like a strangulated cat.

YOUNG MAN: The things you find. Toys, potato mashers, football trophies. I spent an afternoon doing a jigsaw, sticking together these bits of paper. I would've fucking cried if I wasn't laughing. An afternoon doing that bollocks. That's when you know it's getting to you. Time to get out, boy, and no doubt.

HUGH: But I think a bit of culture keeps the head in order.

YOUNG MAN: A birth certificate, a love letter and a fucking tax bill.

HUGH: And a man needs an outside interest. I suppose you could call it a hobby.

YOUNG WOMAN: Pastime, diversion, leisure activity.

YOUNG MAN: Just that. No more. What's that to say for someone's life?

HUGH: Mary sees it as a swizz.

YOUNG MAN: A birth certificate, a love letter and a fucking...

HUGH: She didn't complain the first year we had it. Paid the licence, stuck up the aerial. Twelve months later she was all for burying it in the field. I caught her with the shovel.

YOUNG MAN: 'My darling, you must remember – there is no fear, only love.'

HUGH: She'd already dug the hole.

YOUNG MAN: Fuck.

HUGH: She'd got a letter, a demand for another television licence. 'But haven't we already bought one of them?' She was convinced it was a con.

YOUNG MAN: I shouldn't have read it, but I did.

HUGH: Took me an age to persuade her to keep it.

YOUNG MAN: There is no fear, only love…

HUGH: Used up all of my ingenuity –

YOUNG WOMAN: – Cleverness, skill, shrewdness, cunning.

YOUNG MAN: …What kind of shite is that? No fear only…

HUGH: – Convinced her it'd be all right if we kept a cloth over it. Said the metal detectors couldn't find it so there'd never be a fine.

YOUNG MAN: …Love.

HUGH: She does be frightened of being taken to court. All them gawping at her. She doesn't like to be looked at. I have trouble enough meself and I think I'm married to her.

YOUNG MAN: Saying it like a mantra, a fucking prayer in some ditch –

HUGH: But since when was there a detector van coming up this way?

YOUNG MAN: There is no fear only love, there is no fear only love.

HUGH: Since when was there anything?

YOUNG MAN: Sweating in my own fucking filth in some fucking hole sorting out someone else's fucking problem.

HUGH: You would get the odd ice cream van in the summer. The young one would nip out for a Mr Frosty and three 99s.

YOUNG MAN: There is no fear only love, there is no fear only love, there is no fear only love

HUGH: She liked the blue flavour Mr Frosty. Mary said it looked like anti-freeze.

YOUNG MAN: There is no fear only love, there is no fear only love, there is no fear only love

HUGH: Would turn her teeth green and her tongue black but there was no stopping her.

YOUNG MAN: There is no fear only love, there is no fear only love, there is no fear only love

HUGH: She said it tasted like

YOUNG WOMAN: Pillow cases

HUGH: drying on the line, but there was no telling her.

YOUNG MAN: There is no fear only love, there is no fear only love, there is no fear only love

HUGH: She could talk the hind leg off a donkey and ate dictionaries for breakfast.

YOUNG MAN: There is no fear only love, there is no love only fear, there is no love only fear

HUGH: But the dust settled on that road and it hasn't been raised since.

YOUNG MAN: There is no love only fear, there is no love only fear, there is no love only fear

HUGH: And I got to keep my telly.

YOUNG MAN: There is no love, only fear, there is no love, only fear.

YOUNG WOMAN: Once, I thought I knew who I was, but then I saw it was all relative.

MARY enters with OLD MAN.

MARY: There, now.

HUGH quickly switches off the television before MARY sees but he is not fast enough. She gives him a cool glance as she helps OLD MAN across the room towards his makeshift bed, he high-stepping and awkward.

OLD MAN: One foot, one foot.

MARY: All but had me arse over tip with his making of water, but at least the internal plumbing's in order.

OLD MAN: Step, step.

MARY: No more doing it in the rice pudding tin for you. Outside, like the rest of us, and be glad of it.

OLD MAN: Step, stop.

He stops, carefully reaches down and picks up a feather YOUNG WOMAN has plucked. He touches it, runs his cheek along the feather, looks about and sees the dead carcass. Immediately he becomes distressed.

Pretties, my pretties…

YOUNG WOMAN covers the bird with a tea cloth as MARY takes him forcefully towards his bed, trying to soothe him. He sits, quietened, but not consoled.

The bird has triggered something in him – knowledge, perhaps a memory. He mumbles to himself inaudibly, nodding in agreement.

MARY: For an old man he does have a good bit of life about him. Thought I was at a barn dance with all his dosey-doeing.

YOUNG WOMAN: Shall I make a pot?

MARY: Indeed. I have such a thirst on me it'd slay the dead.

YOUNG WOMAN moves to put on the kettle. MARY sits.

And a cup for the young one there. I'd say he has a head
on him all right after the whack of the jug.
Has he introduced himself yet? Given a title?
A form of address?

*OLD MAN speaks clearly and audibly but no-one
acknowledges his words.*

OLD MAN: The one thing never to give is your name.

Beat.

There is power in knowing a name.

Beat.

They can call you then and when they do, there's no
disobeying.

MARY: So nothing yet, ha?

OLD MAN: You have to answer. No choice in it at all. And
when they have you they'll bury you deep in the hill and
there's no coming back, boy. No coming back at all.

*YOUNG MAN quietly reacts to OLD MAN's words. The
others continue without acknowledging they hear.*

MARY: And well enough to you in here lazing with that
cruel one.

HUGH: Callas.

OLD MAN: And they'll work you to death, they will, and
feed you their slops.

YOUNG WOMAN: Four sugars.

OLD MAN: And in the real world, they'll never forget you, an extra place set at dinner in case you'll walk in the door with the wind caught up in your hair.

MARY: Giving you ideas.

HUGH: It's only opera, Mary.

MARY: Exactly.

OLD MAN: And the mourning will never be over, for there's not so much as a body to bury.

YOUNG MAN: Lines of them, lying in a trench.

OLD MAN: And the grieving will continue until the breath stops short in the mouth

YOUNG MAN: In stadiums, forests, under a football pitch. Jaws kicked in, no use for dental records.

OLD MAN: And then there'll be nobody left to remember their name.

YOUNG WOMAN distributes tea. A beat as she, MARY and HUGH taste it.

OLD MAN and YOUNG MAN sit silently, listening to the after-effect of their words. They do not hear the others.

HUGH: Do you think 'Alan' will do?

MARY: That sugar's too sweet.

YOUNG WOMAN: I put in four.

MARY: But were they heaped or level?

YOUNG WOMAN: Both.

MARY: There is, you know, a world of difference between a level teaspoon and one that is heaped.

YOUNG WOMAN: Some were levelled, some were heaped.

HUGH: So will it, Mary?

YOUNG WOMAN: I didn't know which you preferred, so I gave you two of each.

HUGH: 'Alan'?

MARY: I suppose one word is as good as another.

HUGH: So it's Alan, then.

Beat.

Hello, Alan.

Beat.

Do you remember, Mary, d'you remember when one of the young ones – Alan his name was – d'you remember when one of them – a youngster, now – donkey's years ago – d'you remember when young Alan used to think he was one of them animals off a programme on TV? He'd be skipping in the yard and jumping about – never knew what animal he was supposed to be – but him there dancing and jumping and being an animal and me thinking Christ, isn't it great now to be a child? Isn't it just great to be alive when you're a child with his dancing and his laughing and the jumping and not a bother on him. Not. A. Bother. At all. And me thinking now isn't that great? Isn't that just the greatest thing? Do you remember? And his little smiling face. Split, it was, with the joy. The joy from nothing but being an animal from a programme on TV. Great, ha?
D'you remember, Mary?

A beat

MARY: I'll take them level from now on.

YOUNG WOMAN: Four level.

MARY: Or two heaped.

End of scene.

4

Several days later.

YOUNG MAN still sits on the floor, his hands are bound before him, but his feet are now free. His hair has been tidied, brushed. HUGH reads an out of date newspaper on a hard-backed chair. As he turns a page, the chair wobbles. MARY brushes YOUNG WOMAN's hair.

MARY: My mother used to do this.
    Would near send me to sleep with the sense of it all.

HUGH rests the paper on his lap and shifts on his chair, making it wobble.

I'd muss me hair up special just to have a few minutes longer.
Her undoing the knots.
Releasing all care.

HUGH takes the chair and looks sideways at it, seeing the leg is coming loose at the joint.

I'm lying.

HUGH wobbles the chair.

She'd twang it up in an old elastic band that'd split the hair and spoil the shine.

HUGH tries hitting the joint back in with his fist. He is not successful.

Lumps sticking out everywhere.
Said it was unhealthy to have the pleasure, so she'd send me out looking a right Mary Bangers instead.

HUGH lies the chair on its back, putting his weight on the front legs.

When I was old enough I cut it all off, to spite her.
No more of that for me, no sir.

HUGH bangs the chair with his hand and rights it.

I do think it made her cry.

He hits it and the back legs fall off. He looks at the pieces of debris.

It was something I'd always dreamed of. A Mother brushing a daughter's hair. It was in all the books. I suppose it was meant.

HUGH exits.

I tried doing it for my own young one, but after she was an infant she couldn't bear anyone fussing with her hair. She said she was a big girl now and she knew – indeed she did – she knew all the good styles and what did I know? I was just her useless Mammy.

HUGH enters with a hammer.

YOUNG WOMAN: Did that hurt you?

MARY: Ah, now.

HUGH tries piecing the chair together, hammer in hand, but fails. He puts down the hammer, lines up the chair correctly but cannot reach the hammer.

There were plenty more woundings more deep than that little stab.

He tries again but fails.

The heart is a powerful organ.

HUGH moves the wreckage nearer to the YOUNG MAN on the floor. With his bound hand he tries to steady the chair leg as HUGH lines it up. HUGH raises the hammer but the chair collapses again.

It sustains.

MARY begins to French plait YOUNG WOMAN's hair.

It's always the last to go.

HUGH unties one of YOUNG MAN's hands. He flexes it, then tries to hold the chair leg better. They fail.

At times I do think, though I know I oughtn't, but I do.

Beat.

At times I do think I'm being eaten from the insides out.

HUGH unties YOUNG MAN completely. He stretches, flexing his wrists.

Spleen, liver, guts.

YOUNG WOMAN: Internal organs digesting themselves

MARY: But the heart is always the last to go.

YOUNG MAN and HUGH engross themselves in fixing the chair.

Cruel.
It could be bearable if that went first but no, the storehouse keeps its memories, keeps its beatings, keeps it all in its keep.

YOUNG WOMAN: And it beats and it beats

MARY: Battered.

MARY completes the plait, then undoes it.

I do prefer it down on you.

The men complete the chair and YOUNG MAN gingerly sits on it. It collapses. MARY hoiks him up by the elbow, turns over the chair, pieces it together and gives it a hard bang with the hammer. It is fixed. She rights it.

There.
Useless, the pair of you.

She sets the chair back at the table, throws a tablecloth across it and begins laying out bread, jam, milk and butter for tea. YOUNG WOMAN brings cups and plates to the table. Finally MARY places a covered plate in the centre. She takes off the cloth to reveal the skeleton of a cooked chicken. All but YOUNG MAN sit and begin picking the last of the meat off the carcass. MARY sees YOUNG MAN standing aside, unsure.

And well enough you standing there like a gom. Fetch the tea over, you know where the pot's kept.

The YOUNG MAN gets the teapot. He wavers, uncertain.

Sit down, you make the place look untidy.

He joins them at the table. MARY surveys the spread with satisfaction.

Now.

They begin to pour tea and eat in earnest.

HUGH: Mary does like a bit of company when she eats.

MARY: I do.

HUGH: I often think she'd go on famine if there weren't another mouth to feed.

MARY: Indeed.

HUGH: She wouldn't bother.

MARY: I would not.

HUGH: If she was alone she'd starve.

MARY: Going to all that bother just for one. It isn't natural.

HUGH: Wouldn't be bothered to lift an elbow to saw the bread.

MARY: It's a waste to the day.

HUGH: Isn't there plenty other things for her to be doing other than baking and cooking and peeling spuds?

MARY: There is.

HUGH: She'd die of the hunger.

MARY: Ah.

HUGH: Find a little bag of bones piled tidily away and that'd be Mary.
Deceased.

MARY: I think you've made your point now and let that be the end to it.

A pause. MARY stares at the YOUNG MAN.

Did your Mother never teach you any manners?
We'll have no elbows on tables in this house.

YOUNG MAN takes his arms from the table. HUGH takes the last pre-cut slice of bread and spoons jam onto it, smoothing it on. YOUNG MAN reaches for the uncut soda bread. He takes out an army knife, opening the blade to slice the bread. All become still. MARY clicks her fingers at him and holds out her open hand to him. YOUNG MAN passes her the knife. She snaps it closed and pockets it.

I'll have nothing sharp under my roof.
There's enough things as it is that'd cut you to the bone without having them to hand, inviting trouble.

She stands, turns her back and takes out a large bread knife on a string from about her neck. She slices the bread and returns the knife to beneath her clothing. She offers the YOUNG MAN the plate of sliced bread.

There, now.

HUGH: It always tastes better when someone else has done the work.

YOUNG MAN: We'd walk into houses sometimes and the food would still be on the table. Knife and fork crossed on the plate, like they'd only put them down for a minute to get a drink from the other room. Potato, meat, the gravy with a skin grown over it.

HUGH: That jam turned out well.

YOUNG MAN: In one there was the remains of a birthday party. Eight candles sitting on a cake. She never got to open the presents, nor play Blind Man's Bluff, Musical Chairs. She'd blown out the candles, though. The wicks were black and hardly any wax spilt on the icing. But she'd blown out the candles.

YOUNG WOMAN: And maybe made her wish.

HUGH: Is it the quality of the fruit in it, Mary? Is it that that has it so good?

YOUNG MAN: They must have left in a hurry. The minimum of packing. Load everything up in the car. Sometimes they're sent drivers with trucks.

MARY: A bit of fruit and sugar will taste good to any old fool.

YOUNG MAN: It's called assisting with voluntary relocation. Being neighbourly and they don't charge too much for the petrol.

HUGH starts eating the jam straight from the jar.

Sometimes they travel separately. Women silent at the destination, the men yet to arrive.

HUGH: That jam, now, is mighty.

YOUNG MAN: Being told to be patient, there was a diversion, a delay.

Pause.

They'll have a long fucking wait.

MARY: Language.

HUGH: It's better, that, than what my mother did make.

MARY: I'll not have canteen slang in my kitchen.

MARY takes the jam pot from HUGH.

And you've had enough of that, now. It'll give you worms.

HUGH stares at her, then starts reading again the out of date newspaper.

But she blew out the candles, you say?
Blew them out, the top of the cake?

Beat.

Ah, well, that's something, at least.

YOUNG WOMAN: I always wished to be someone else when it was my turn. Sometimes I'd demand to blow them out twice, just to be sure. Then one day I woke up and it'd happened.
I don't wish now.

A beat. HUGH rattles his newspaper, eventually folds it and puts it down.

HUGH: It's a waste of time. It's an old one, I know it by heart.
Mary, could I not have another ration – a little bit of print to read?

MARY considers, then goes to a cupboard where she takes out several cups, bundled in newspaper. She unwraps them and hands the creased balls of paper to YOUNG MAN.

MARY: Pass that over to y'man, will you?

She tidies away the cups. YOUNG MAN smooths out some of the newspaper, noticing the date.

YOUNG MAN: It's years old.

MARY: What harm?
Indeed, it's better not to know.

YOUNG MAN gives HUGH the pieces of newspaper. He begins laboriously ironing them out with his hand, putting them in order to make a semblance of a newspaper. YOUNG MAN watches on.

YOUNG MAN: Even the crossword's filled in.

A beat.

YOUNG WOMAN: I wanted to be a good girl, tried to be caring.
Thought the cupboard was filled with plenty. Gave out armfuls – 'Here, take it, take…' All those hands, open with want. Never thought I'd need anything for myself.

MARY: You can get by and make do, if you put your mind to it hard enough. Can live in a cave, sleep through the winter, so I'm told.

YOUNG WOMAN: I wanted to help. Wished for it.

MARY: Ah! Now.

YOUNG WOMAN: Never thought their despair would seep through into me.
Like mould. Spores of it, thick in the air. You take great lung-fulls in and it settles there, pocking.

MARY: No damage if you use bleach. And water. Plenty of it.
That's the trouble with you young ones. Have no idea of hygiene.

A roar of anguish is heard distantly, off.

YOUNG WOMAN: Their pain goes in like a splinter of glass. No use taking tweezers to it. It has to grow out, breaking the skin, leaving a scar. And it burns. So many shards. You get them just by brushing past people in the street. Their damage hanging out of them like so many icicles. You come home bristled, bleeding from wounds. And it's not even your pain.

Another cry, closer this time.

MARY: It's the little mercies. They can, you know, they can. Yes.
Would break my heart, a cake made and it not used.
But she blew the candles at least and that's some comfort. Not much. But it'll do.

OLD MAN enters quietly, blood on his hands. He stands.

OLD MAN: I warned you, I warned you.

He holds auburn feathers, strokes them.

Pretties. My pretties, all gone.

YOUNG MAN backs away.

YOUNG MAN: First sign.

OLD MAN: All gone, done.

MARY: Hush, now. Sit.

MARY tries to get OLD MAN to sit. He resists.

OLD MAN: All…

MARY: Flown away. We'll find some, you'll see.

She gets him into the chair, starts cleaning him up.

OLD MAN: Warm in my hands. Wet.

MARY: They'll be hid up in the bushes. Anne, pour him a cup of tea.

YOUNG WOMAN complies.

OLD MAN: Gone.

MARY: Not all. They're crafty. Some will have got away.

OLD MAN: Teeth.
  I warned youse.

MARY: We'll send the young ones out later and

YOUNG MAN: – No!

OLD MAN: Stay close, don't go out.

YOUNG MAN: It's a warning. I know. I know it's a –

OLD MAN: Pretties, then –

MARY: – That's enough!

She takes the cup of tea from YOUNG WOMAN and holds it as OLD MAN drinks.

Did you put a good bit of sugar in it, for the shock?

HUGH: I heard of this –

MARY: – Hugh!

He withdraws.

YOUNG MAN: First, kill the hens, then kill the livestock and they come for –

MARY: – I'll have none of that talk! It was a fox.

OLD MAN: Punishment.

MARY: A fox.

OLD MAN rejects the tea.

OLD MAN: We built in the wrong place.

YOUNG MAN: Their land.

MARY: Ours.

YOUNG MAN: They'll take it back.

MARY: Stop it.

YOUNG MAN: If you take one of their plots, they'll have you.

OLD MAN: Will wait, a long time, if need be.

YOUNG MAN: But they'll have you.

MARY: Jesus, am I the only one here with any sense?

YOUNG MAN: They don't like us being here.

MARY: I've never heard such nonsense…

OLD MAN: They set traps. Not for animals, no.

MARY: That's it, into the bed.

She guides OLD MAN towards the makeshift bed.

OLD MAN: And you get stuck in them traps and you can't step out.

MARY: It's the shock.

OLD MAN: A fella I know, he told me.

MARY: Oh yes, the self-same fella went dancing with the little people and rode on the back of a unicorn.

She tries to settle him on the bed.

OLD MAN: You'll see.

MARY: Don't be making any promises you can't keep.

OLD MAN: It's sacred. Their soil.

MARY: And who tends it? Who feeds it? Who cleared it of stones, the pail growing heavy in the hand?

OLD MAN: From their history, ancient times.

MARY: So who looks after it? Who loves it?
Us.
Breaking the husk of the soil and it frozen, to make life
come through. Watering it when there's a drought,
building channels to irrigate... Us. If it's anyone else's
plot I wouldn't mind them coming and giving me a hand
with it. I'm weary with the tending of it. And Jesus, I'm
worse than a child to be arg'ing with you.

OLD MAN: It's –

MARY: – Our land and I'll have no more of your stories.
From any of you.

*MARY clears the table by taking up the ends of the tablecloth
in her hand and lifting it, filled with utensils and crockery,
clear off the table. Teatime is over. YOUNG MAN and
WOMAN stand, afraid.*

A long, tense silence.

HUGH: Did you see the fox, Mary?
I think I saw the fox.

End of scene.

5

Twenty months before Scene 1.

The kitchen is warm, comfortable, fairly prosperous; a state reflected in dress. The concert of Maria Callas in Hamburg 1959 plays loudly, in all its richness, on CD. HUGH sits at the table doing a crossword in the paper, YOUNG MAN lies on the floor, his head in the cupboard under the sink. YOUNG WOMAN enters with potatoes in a pot. She sees YOUNG MAN under the sink, kicks his outstretched foot – there is no reaction. Warily she begins to peel the potatoes into a bowl, keeping an eye on the prostrate figure.

HUGH twitches the paper, clicks his tongue and sighs. He begins to address YOUNG WOMAN, then changes his mind, his voice barely audible owing to the volume of the CD.

HUGH: Do you – ah, no. No.

He returns to the paper, reading the crossword puzzle silently, moving his lips. Frustrated, he goes to address YOUNG WOMAN again, changes his mind.

– no…no. D'you – ? Nothing.

He disappears again into the puzzle. MARY enters, pulling on a working jacket, on her way outside. As she passes through, she switches off the opera, coinciding with HUGH's exasperation as he throws the paper away from him. His words come out unintentionally loud.

Fekkin' stupid anyway. How's a body supposed to…

YOUNG WOMAN: What?

HUGH: Ah, nothing.

MARY exits.

HUGH: Bloody daft, stupid yolk.

YOUNG WOMAN: Are you stuck with the puzzles again?

HUGH: How's a b – I am not. No. But how's a body supposed to understand this – jabber – nonsense…

YOUNG WOMAN: Ask me. I might know.

HUGH: Ha!

YOUNG WOMAN: Go on.

HUGH: I will not.

YOUNG WOMAN: Suit yourself.
　　Just thought I could help.

HUGH: (*Quickly.*) D'you know what a lignite is?

YOUNG WOMAN: A – ?

HUGH: Thought as much. See, I told you.

YOUNG WOMAN: Spell it.

HUGH: Aaah… Got you. Got you thinking now, haven't I? Maybe you're not as cute as you thought.

YOUNG WOMAN: I couldn't hear. You rushed it.

HUGH: It's not important anyway. Just an oul rag, trading people's misery, calling it news.

YOUNG MAN: (*From beneath sink.*) Lignite.

YOUNG WOMAN: What?

HUGH: There's a story here, now – a story that's a horror story, that's what it is – and they're masquerading it as news, as entertainment.

YOUNG MAN: (*Under sink.*) L-I-G-N-I-T-E.

HUGH: Some fella out on the razzle lost his keys and was so late home the missus had gone to bed, locking him out.

YOUNG WOMAN: 'Lignite'?

HUGH: Are you listening to this story or am I talking to the table?

YOUNG WOMAN: Listening.

She dries her hands, goes towards the cupboard, begins sorting through it.

HUGH: So he's banging on the door and the missus isn't answering – she's up, snoring her head off in the bed – and the quare fella's outside, not fancying a night shivering in the coal shed.

YOUNG WOMAN finds an old dictionary and starts flicking through it.

So doesn't the clever article only come up with the idea that if he can set the fire alarm off, he'll wake her and she'll let him in…?

She stops looking in the book.

YOUNG WOMAN: I don't think I want to hear this.

HUGH: So doesn't the bollix for brains only siphon off some petrol from the car…

YOUNG WOMAN: No…

HUGH: Tip it through the letterbox and follow it up with a match?

YOUNG WOMAN: Jesus.

HUGH: Set the fire alarm off all right. Whole place burnt to the ground. Barbecued wife.

YOUNG MAN gets up from under sink.

YOUNG WOMAN: I don't belie…

YOUNG MAN: (*Sarcastically.*) It has to be true, it's in the papers. (*To HUGH.*) Isn't that right? But then again, you just read the funnies and the crossword, don't you? And swallow the crap of the editorial, hook line and sinker. Sure, the economy's fine and equality's the name of the game...

HUGH: (*Interrupting.*) Did you find the word?

YOUNG WOMAN: Read the clue.

HUGH: 'Hard black variety of lignite; spurt, stream, plane.' Three letters.

YOUNG WOMAN: Jet. It is, isn't it? Jet plane, jet of water, jet precious stone... So who's the cute hoor now?

HUGH: Mind your mouth, girl.

YOUNG MAN: It doesn't count if you look it up in the dictionary.

YOUNG WOMAN: I don't care.
Go on, ask me another.

HUGH: Try the tap first.

YOUNG MAN takes up his position again under the sink as YOUNG WOMAN turns on the tap. The water splashes all over him. HUGH is delighted.

YOUNG MAN: Shit.

HUGH: You forgot to put the u-bend back, soft lad.

He starts drying himself and mopping the floor.

YOUNG MAN: I don't see you volunteering to do any graft – just sit on your arse and give advice after the fact.

Silence. YOUNG WOMAN tries to salvage the mood.

YOUNG WOMAN: Another, go on...

YOUNG MAN: It's cheating if you look at the dictionary.

HUGH makes himself absent, although still present.

YOUNG WOMAN: Who's judging?

YOUNG MAN: If you're going to do something, you should do it right, not cut corners.

YOUNG WOMAN: It's only a crossword...

YOUNG MAN: But that's how it begins.

YOUNG WOMAN: What?

YOUNG MAN: Erosion.
Be careful. It's all in the detail.

She pushes him away.

MARY enters, pulling off rubber boots.

MARY: That nag'll have to go. She's lame, has arthritis and the cataracts are that big on her eyes they're like saucers.

YOUNG WOMAN: Rosie? Go where?

MARY: Where d'you think?

YOUNG MAN: Bang-bang time.

YOUNG WOMAN: Oh...

MARY: Don't be giving me the poor mouth and the lip quivering. I told you when we got her: she's a working horse, not a pet. Was only a cheap replacement for the tractor and now she's costing more than she earns.

YOUNG WOMAN: But –

MARY: No buts.

HUGH becomes present again as MARY addresses him.

(*To HUGH.*) I told you it'd be a mistake letting her go giving it a love name. Rosie. Jesus, did you ever hear such a stupid name for a nag? I said we should have kept it simple: 'Tractor'. There'd be no getting fond of it with a mechanical name.

YOUNG WOMAN: But it's a she and she's alive and she's real…

MARY: (*To HUGH.*) Now look at the trouble you've started. If we hadn't christened the horse, there'd be no attachment.

YOUNG WOMAN: Of course there would. It's Rosie, it's –

YOUNG MAN: Sink's unblocked.

MARY: Ah, there's my good lad.

YOUNG WOMAN: You can't just…

MARY: …I can and I will and that's the end of it. (*To HUGH.*) Or rather, you will.

HUGH: What?

MARY: You can't get out of your duties that easy.

HUGH: But Mary…

MARY: …You're worse than the girl.

YOUNG MAN: I'll do it.

They speak aside to one another.

YOUNG WOMAN: You would.

YOUNG MAN: Be good practice.

YOUNG WOMAN: For what?

YOUNG MAN: Life.

YOUNG WOMAN: And what else?

YOUNG MAN: Shut it.

MARY hears, reacts to the tensions.

MARY: What?

YOUNG MAN: It was tea leaves, you know. That's what blocked the sink. Disgusting. All mangled and shitty and –

MARY: Language.

YOUNG MAN: It's a really dirty habit. And in the stone ages. What's wrong with teabags?

MARY: I know, I do say, but –

HUGH: – You can taste the paper from them things. Blindfolded, give me a cup made with a bag and a cup made properly, in a pot and I could tell the difference.

YOUNG MAN: Sure.

HUGH: Just by smelling.

They speak aside to each other again.

YOUNG WOMAN: That was very clever, wasn't it?

YOUNG MAN: Huh?

YOUNG WOMAN: You know.

MARY: What?

YOUNG MAN: Stirrer.

MARY: The spuds not even finished and her there with her words and her books.

HUGH: Humour her, what harm?
  They can take your house and all your possessions, but they can never take your education from you.

YOUNG MAN: Who's 'they'?

HUGH: Them, they, people, whoever. You know.

YOUNG MAN: No I don't.

HUGH: It's a generalisation. Vague.

YOUNG MAN: So it's not political?

HUGH: Them – they – who – ever.

YOUNG MAN: You're not commenting on the state of current affairs?

MARY: – Christ almighty! I do sometimes think, I do, that –

YOUNG MAN: – Once, you could be proud of this country.

MARY: I'll finish the potatoes!

YOUNG MAN: It had standing in the world – respected – people were respected.

He speaks, as MARY peels the spuds, YOUNG WOMAN crosses to a bookshelf and gets her thesaurus, HUGH reads his newspaper. OLD MAN enters, crosses and washes his hands at the sink.

But like a virus, a disease – infecting our water, poisoning the very air we breathe – suddenly we weren't all brothers – suddenly some were the leaders and others the led. And who decided this? The same portion who, by dint of birth, claim privilege is theirs – culture, education – the very genes in their cells are superior, or so they say.

OLD MAN gets himself a glass of water. He drinks it standing up, looking out across the fields with satisfaction. He exits.

And because they own the newspapers, that's what's printed and because they own the radio stations, that's what's in the air and because they own the factories, only they get promoted and because they are the military, it's time that we prepare.
Because if we don't make our own strategies – we're an endangered species.

YOUNG WOMAN looks up from comparing an entry in the dictionary with the thesaurus.

YOUNG WOMAN: I've got a new word from the dictionary.

MARY: Christ almighty! I do –

HUGH: Sssh. Leave her, Mary.

YOUNG WOMAN: Here.

She thrusts the book at YOUNG MAN.

This is just for you.
Belligerent….nationalistic…

He throws down the book and starts to walk out.

…militant…warlike…

YOUNG MAN exits, slamming the door behind him.

HUGH: How many letters?

YOUNG WOMAN: Eight.

HUGH: Any other clues?

YOUNG WOMAN: It comes from a nineteenth century conjuring term.

MARY: So come and conjure me up some carrots, ha?

YOUNG WOMAN: I will. By jingo.

There is a loud shot outside. They stop dead, still.

Several beats.

YOUNG MAN enters, clattering down a twelve bore on to the table.

YOUNG MAN: I've fixed the tractor.

He throws himself down in a chair, looks at HUGH.

End of scene.

6

Several weeks after Scene 5.

It is YOUNG WOMAN's birthday. Throughout the scene, MARY is making preparations for her birthday tea. She stops or hides the activity whenever YOUNG WOMAN is present.

HUGH is looking through seed catalogues; MARY takes bread out of the oven. YOUNG WOMAN breaks some off immediately, then heads outside.

MARY: The amount of bread she wastes…

A beat.

MARY takes out a birthday cake from under the sink.

Does she think I have nothing better to be doing than kneading dough that she may squander on them birds?

She takes birthday candles from her pocket and candle holders hidden in a packet of corn flour in the cupboard.

Some of them are the size of pullets.

She begins putting the candles in their holders on the cake.

Aren't they out there now in the field, gorging themselves on the good seed we did sow?

Beat.

So plump their wings can't carry them.

Several beats.

The cats'll get them, you'll see.

Beat.

Or the stoats and weasels.

HUGH: Did you hear that fox barking again last night?

MARY: Indeed. And it'll come closer if it gets a sniff of them bantams.

HUGH: Ah, it'll go for the fat sparrows first. There may be method yet in the young one's madness.

MARY: And tears before bedtime, if –

HUGH: (*Interrupting.*) – Don't be getting on at her today. Tomorrow will do, but not today.

Where's the lad?

MARY: Out.

HUGH: Another one of his 'meetings'?

MARY: He'll be back in time. I told him.

HUGH rattles his seed catalogue, displaying his displeasure.

He's only going to listen.

Beat.

Taking an interest in the world.

Beat.

More than you ever did.
And don't look at me like that. I do have a pain in me head from you looking at me like that.

HUGH: So put it back in the sand, why don't you?

MARY: And there's no need to be taking the face off me.

HUGH: He shouldn't be getting involved in…

MARY: …Ah, hush. Anyone'd think there was trouble, the way you go on.

HUGH: Do you not listen to the radio, pay attention to the news?

MARY: So long as there's food on the table, a roof over our head and corn in the field, everything's fine.

HUGH: And there was that palaver in the city, trouble on the border and you don't even want to think about what the papers say…

MARY: …That's just as well because I've cancelled them. Save you the bother.

HUGH: Mary, do you have any idea…!

MARY: (*Overlapping.*) …It doesn't help to be mithering, so I've put paid to it.

(*Sole voice.*) If we were meant to think more we'd…

She realises, stops and looks at HUGH. They exchange a long look, unbroken even as YOUNG WOMAN enters slowly, backwards, dropping crumbs of bread.

Several beats.

MARY throws a cloth over the cake, hiding it. She takes up a cloth as Scene 1, and begins embroidering it. YOUNG WOMAN drops to her knees, making low encouraging noises, throwing crumbs of bread. MARY recovers.

Jesus, it's the babes in the wood in reverse.

YOUNG WOMAN: Sssh. Come on…

OLD MAN enters through the door, carrying a pail of hen meal. YOUNG WOMAN leaps to her feet in annoyance.

You and your bloody big feet!

MARY: Anne!

There is no real anger between OLD MAN and YOUNG WOMAN, just a pleasurable bickering – their interaction is part chiding, part indulgence.

YOUNG WOMAN: I've spent days trying to get it indoors.
I nearly have it and –

OLD MAN: – There's plenty of feathers in the hen house.
Have you lost interest in them all ready?

YOUNG WOMAN: No.

OLD MAN: So why are they still cooped up in the hen
house? Scratching in their own shit, not a drop of water
in the pen. I wouldn't have built the shagging thing if I'd
known you couldn't look after them.

YOUNG WOMAN: I can. It's just not the same as taming a
wild bird. They have a hard life, need help even more.

MARY: She'd have them eating off the whiskers of a fox.

OLD MAN: Hens earn their keep. Fresh eggs, every
morning.
What would a robin offer you?

YOUNG WOMAN: Luck.

MARY: Not in the house, it wouldn't.

YOUNG WOMAN: But you said they were lucky.

MARY: Out in the garden, maybe, but not in the house. A
robin in the house brings death.

*YOUNG MAN enters, the temper up in him, pockets filled
with leaflets.*

OLD MAN: Its breast was splashed with the Christ's blood
when it tried to pluck a thorn from his brow, so they say,
All robins have carried the stain since. The bleeding
breast, the lacerated heart.

YOUNG MAN: No wonder the place is going to the dogs.

They notice him. Pause.

Fable and superstition.

OLD MAN: Ah, if it's fables you want…

OLD MAN tries to smooth over the tautening atmosphere, addressing YOUNG WOMAN. The conversations occur simultaneously.

HUGH: I see you've come back in a good mood.

MARY: Hugh.

YOUNG MAN: So would you if you'd heard half of what I just did. You'd be ashamed to be sitting on your fat arse…

MARY: Alan!

YOUNG MAN: …doing nothing, as usual. You don't know what's going on out there.

HUGH: I read the papers –

YOUNG MAN: That's bollocks! It's party line, censored, and I'm not going to take it anymore.

OLD MAN: The little people, now, they're a fabled tribe. But they have no hearts. No feeling whatsoever.

No compassion.

They're vicious wee bastards. Would stick a pin in your eye and laugh at your pain… And if you say you don't believe in them, they'll teach you a lesson all right, out of spite.

Parallel dialogue ends.

YOUNG MAN: Look at you! Embroidering altar cloths and him – telling fairy stories and she's eighteen years old.

YOUNG WOMAN: Thanks for remembering. I didn't get your card, but I'm sure you've been too busy with other, more weighty concerns...

YOUNG MAN: Like planning a birthday party?

I thought you wanted to help, make a difference...

YOUNG WOMAN: I do. It's just...

Chastened, her words fade away to nothing.

YOUNG MAN: You're as bad as him. All mouth, no action.

MARY: (*Quietly.*) That's enough.

YOUNG MAN: We've been under their thumb for too long.

Who has the best jobs, education, housing?

MARY: Son...

YOUNG MAN: And who's just sat there, pathetic, and not done any(thing)...

HUGH begins to exit.

...Don't walk away from me!

HUGH: I'll speak with you when you're calm. Until then...

YOUNG MAN: ...That's right, run away, like your generation always have.

YOUNG WOMAN: Please...(don't)

HUGH: Mary, call me when you're making tea.

YOUNG MAN: You've always been cowards.

Too scared to speak up for your rights...

HUGH: ...And I'm not going to be bullied into them, either.

YOUNG MAN: There will be a time for action and when it arrives I'll be ready.

HUGH exits.

MARY: (*Matter of fact.*) Son, you couldn't find your cock in the dark, let alone pee straight.

YOUNG MAN exits outside. A beat. MARY examines the cloth then bundles it into a ball

(*Ironically.*) No more of that. Altar cloth or not, it does be hard on the eyes. I shan't have it out again until it's ready to be my shroud, then I can go to the maker with 'I have suffered' sewn in all around each side.

She puts the cloth away into her sewing basket, then into a cupboard.

An uneasy silence. YOUNG WOMAN stands apart.

OLD MAN tries to lighten the mood and draw YOUNG WOMAN back to him.

OLD MAN: (*Lightly sarcastic.*) Is he a changeling, Mary? Did the Little People swap the real Alan with one of their own?

MARY: Ah, some such.

She begins preparing tea and setting the table, OLD MAN starts winding YOUNG WOMAN in.

OLD MAN: For they're terrible vindictive if they think you've done them a wrong.

A beat.

YOUNG WOMAN: Like what?

A beat.

OLD MAN: Trespassing on their land…spying on them…
picking up something they did drop…
And the one thing you must never do is let them know
your name. For they'll call you if they know how to
name you, and you have to answer, for it's fierce strong
magic. It's like you're hypnotised. And they'll carry you
away into their fairy fort and make you do all their dirty
work until the moment you drop down, dead.

MARY: I do think the young lad had a point. Look at you
there, turning her brains to jam.

*MARY tries ruffling her hair, YOUNG WOMAN pushes
her off.*

YOUNG WOMAN: I hate that.

MARY: You and your children's stories.

OLD MAN: It's part of her culture, her heritage. If she
doesn't know that, how will she recognise herself?

MARY: By looking in a mirror.

Call your Father.

*YOUNG WOMAN exits. MARY uncovers the birthday cake
and begins lighting the candles. OLD MAN puts on traditional
music. As YOUNG WOMAN enters, HUGH following, he
places a blindfold over her eyes. OLD MAN takes her in his
arms and leads her in a dance. She laughs, stumbling. He
helps her by naming the steps. HUGH catches MARY after
she has placed the cake on the table and dances with her.*

OLD MAN: One foot in front of the other, another foot
before the other, step, step, lightly step, plod. One foot,
the other foot, one foot soft to the earth, step, move, step
forward now, not long. Stand. Breathe. One foot crosses
the other, another foot before the other…

He stops, as do HUGH and MARY. YOUNG MAN is standing before them in a soldier's uniform, holding a gun, aimed at them. YOUNG WOMAN is oblivious, laughing. Still blindfolded, she finds her way to the table and the burning candles. She stands before them.

YOUNG WOMAN: I wish… I wish….

She blows out the candles.

Black out.

The sound of distant artillery.

End.